INSTITUTE FOR RESEARCH INTO MENTAL RETARDATION

SYMPOSIUM NO. 1

RESIDENTIAL CARE FOR THE MENTALLY RETARDED

RESIDENTIAL CARE FOR THE MENTALLY RETARDED

A Symposium held at the Middlesex Hospital Medical School on 28th November 1968 under the auspices of the Institute for Research into Mental Retardation, London

EDITED BY

Elspeth Stephen, MA, DipEd

Principal Psychologist,
Queen Mary's Hospital for Children, Carshalton

SYMPOSIUM NO. 1

PUBLISHED FOR THE
INSTITUTE FOR RESEARCH INTO MENTAL RETARDATION BY

PERGAMON PRESS

Oxford · New York · Toronto · Sydney · Braunschweig

Pergamon Press Ltd., Headington Hill Hall, Oxford
Pergamon Press Inc., Maxwell House, Fairview Park, Elmsford, New York 10523
Pergamon of Canada Ltd., 207 Queen's Quay West, Toronto 1
Pergamon Press (Aust.) Pty. Ltd., 19a Boundary Street, Rushcutters Bay, N.S.W. 2011, Australia
Vieweg & Sohn GmbH, Burgplatz 1, Braunschweig

First edition 1970

Library of Congress Catalog Card No. 73–117408

Printed in Great Britain by A. Wheaton & Co., Exeter

08 016106 5

Contents

Foreword to Series

MENTAL retardation is a meeting point for all those scientific disciplines which have a bearing upon the study of man. Indeed, as a field for research it sometimes yields knowledge of wider human significance than for the retarded alone, for in them we find in exaggerated or abnormal form—and hence sometimes more readily accessible for study—the ordinary processes of life.

The twin problems of prevention and amelioration of mental handicap form focal points for research in this field; these issues are, however, sometimes less distinct than they sound. Successful amelioration becomes, in effect, prevention. Within all disciplines major discoveries are now taking place and the understanding of causes as well as improvements in treatment have correspondingly advanced. These range from, on the one hand, a better knowledge of the genetics of some rare forms of handicap, and on the other, the initiation of properly controlled programmes of psychosocial intervention which seem likely to prevent the emergence of mild retardation in children heavily at risk. It is already clear that the groundwork for more effective prevention and more successful amelioration is now being laid, although our continuing ignorance on many important matters should not be underestimated. A few examples will suffice: although the problem of phenylketonuria and its treatment have attracted wide publicity, it is becoming increasingly clear that the model upon which such work depended is in need of some revision. Or again, as yet there has been little elucidation of the chain of events that leads from abnormality of genic material to brain anomalies and hence to the mental retardation itself. And finally, the degree to which mild retardation may be reversible by early intervention, and the optimal form of such intervention, remain to be established.

The twin aims of prevention and amelioration will both be well represented in the Symposium Series of the Institute for Research into Mental Retardation. The first Symposium on Residential Care is to be followed by another on Genetic Counselling and a third on Biochemical Screening. The Institute plans to sponsor three such symposia per year on topical subjects within its field of interest. The many facets of relevant research will thus be comprehensively presented over a relatively short period of time, and it is the intention of the sponsors that these symposia should be published soon after taking place so that they may be available in a thoroughly up-to-date form. At a period when all fields are moving forward rapidly, the Symposia are likely to prove valuable to all professional workers with interests in mental retardation.

A. D. B. CLARKE,
Professor of Psychology,
University of Hull and
member of the Research
Committee of the IRMR

Preface

THE residential care of the mentally retarded has for long been a subject for public debate. During the last hundred years it has been a matter which has exercised successive governments which have appointed Royal Commissions, Departmental and Inter-Departmental Committees, and Committees of Inquiry, to guide them on policy or to investigate specific problems. There has been a thin stream of articles in the medical and psychological press reporting surveys by individual doctors, research teams working in social medicine or social psychiatry, and the deliberations of working parties set up by organizations such as the British Psychological Association, the Royal Medico-Psychological Association and local paediatric societies.

These investigations have been for the most part fact-finding (or occasionally muck-raking). Either they have collected evidence upon which to base recommendations regarding policy, or they have ventilated specific criticisms of existing hospital practice. What is conspicuously lacking in the literature on residential care for the subnormal—or indeed for other types of handicapped persons—are analyses of the determinants of patterns of care, and systematic investigations into the factors that influence its quality. Considering mental subnormality as a social and public health problem it is studies of these factors which perhaps hold out most hope for the long-term improvement of our mental deficiency services—and indeed for the better social and personal adjustment of the mentally retarded themselves. The need is for systematic and continuing study, preferably experimental.

The papers in this symposium describe some of the current work on these problems being undertaken in England. They illustrate applications of social science to medicine which go beyond diagnosis or assessment and begin to study processes and the factors which influence them. They are therefore welcome in that they concern themselves with quality as well as type of care, and in that they direct our attention to problems which are of central importance, both theoretically and practically, to the functioning of services.

JACK TIZARD, MA, BLITT, PHD
Professor of Child Development,
Institute of Education,
University of London

Paper No. 1

ALBERT KUSHLICK, MB, BCH, MRCP, DPH

Director of Research in Subnormality, Wessex Regional Hospital Board, Senior Research Officer, Institute of Education, London University and Member of the Research Committee, IRMR

THIS paper is mainly concerned with the need for residential care for the severely subnormal. It is divided into two main sections. It first presents some findings from a survey I and my colleague, Miss Gillian Cox, have recently undertaken in the South of England, on the size and nature of the problem of residential care for SSN subjects. It then describes the major functions of residential care for these people. After a short discussion on possible ways in which these needs may be met, the proposals of Wessex Regional Hospital Board for future services are briefly described, to illustrate how the findings can be applied. The possibility and the need to evaluate different forms of care are stressed.

The second section discusses the quality of care in residential institutions for the mentally handicapped. Some recent data from our researches and those of Professor Tizard and his colleagues are presented. I believe that, taken together with the information on the size of the problem, these data may be useful guides to the provision in the future of adequate facilities providing high quality of care. They also reveal the need for further research into many problems of which we have, as yet, few answers.

In discussing the need for residential care for the retarded, we need to know both what function the institution will perform and, how many of the inmates will, at any time, need the services provided. It is useful to conceive of three basic types of institution.

First, a place which provides continuous skilled medical and nursing care with all of the highly technical and expensive aids for diagnosis and treatment without which people will die, become seriously ill or develop complications of their illnesses.

Second, a place which provides a substitute home for those whose parents cannot for one reason or another cope with them in their own home. The parents of SSN children, and particularly their mothers, are faced with profound problems, not only of coming to terms with the psychological shock of having borne a severely handicapped child, but also of managing on their own, and for 24 hours in the day, a child whose infantile and early childhood behaviour will persist for much longer than in the case of a normal child, and possibly for life. Mothers' problems include those of dealing with incontinence, failure to walk, overactivity and destructiveness for much longer periods than parents of normal children. Added to these burdens are other problems (such as epilepsy, paralysis and extra illnesses). They have been systematically measured and described by Dr. Grad and Professor Tizard.[15] Despite these problems many families are able to cope until some other family crisis like the birth of another child, illness or death in the family, which so adds to the family burden that the parents cannot continue to cope with the handicapped child. In these circumstances, the residential care needed is a substitute home where professional child care staff are able both to cope and to provide the child with the social experiences of a home life it cannot get within its own family. Professional staff can cope because they work a shift system as opposed to mother's 24 hours, and because they have available professional, medical, educational and social work support in specially designed facilities for handicapped subjects.

The third type of care is a combination of a substitute home and legal detention. This type of care is appropriate for people who need both home care and psychiatric or other treatment for their own safety or that of the community, but who are unable or unwilling to accept such treatment voluntarily. This type of care applies almost solely to the MSN adolescents and adults and will not be further discussed in this paper.

A major problem of planning and developing residential care services for the retarded is therefore first to estimate the numbers of SSN people in communities of a particular size. The second part of the exercise is to estimate how many of the people so identified will at any time need the different forms of residential care so far described.

There is now a considerable body of evidence to suggest that the major form of residential care required for SSN children and adults is that of the substitute home type. We also have, at least for Britain, some idea of the extent of such provision required for total population of standard size.

It is certainly true that the interpretations placed on the available evidence are controversial. However, I believe that the controversies concern neither the numbers of places required nor the purpose that these provisions will serve. They concern solely who shall provide and staff them, and the administrative form which the services should take. I will come back to these questions later.

I would now like to present some of the evidence on the size and nature of the problem of providing residential care for SSN children and adults. This arises from a survey I and my colleagues have been conducting into the prevalence of mental retardation in an area of the South of England served by the Wessex Regional Hospital Board.[6] This area includes the County Boroughs of Southampton, Bournemouth and Portsmouth and the Counties of Hampshire, Dorset, the Isle of Wight and part of Wiltshire. It has a total population of about 2 million. Although it includes large areas of rural land, the majority of the population live in urban areas along the South coast. Moreover, the demographic characteristics of the areas are very similar to those of England and Wales, and the findings therefore appear generalizable to the country as a whole. The survey data describe the position as it was on 1st July 1963, but we know from our follow-up data that the position has not changed much since then.

Table 1 shows the social and physical incapacities of the retarded by age (children and adults), by grade (SSN and MSN) and by place of care (institution—Inst.; or living at home—Home).

SSN means severely subnormal, i.e. I.Q. score less than 50.

MSN means mildly subnormal, i.e. I.Q. score 50 and over, mainly 50 to 70.

N-A means non-ambulant.

ALL SB means severely behaviour disorded with or without severe incontinence. These people are, of course, ambulant. The

TABLE 1

AGE, GRADE, SOCIAL AND PHYSICAL INCAPACITY AND PLACE OF CARE (WESSEX REGION 1.7.63. CRUDE RATES/100,000)

Age	Grade	Place of Care	Incapacity—SPI				Total
			N-A	ALL SB	SI	CAN	
Children	SSN	Home	4 (1)	4 (3)	2 (1)	20 (18)	30 (23)
		Inst.	5 (—)	5 (2)	3 (2)	5 (4)	18 (9)
	MSN	Home	1 (—)	1 (1)	1 (—)	7 (6)	9 (7)
		Inst.	— (—)	1 (—)	— (—)	1 (1)	2 (2)
Adults	SSN	Home	2 (1)	2 (1)	1 (—)	45 (19)	51 (20)
		Inst.	6 (1)	14 (3)	6 (1)	54 (19)	81 (24)
	MSN	Home	1 (—)	— (—)	— (—)	70 (10)	76 (10)
		Inst.	2 (1)	4 (2)	1 (—)	45 (16)	53 (18)

behaviour disorders include overactivity, aggression, destructiveness, attention seeking and self-injury.

SI means severely incontinent—i.e. they soil themselves day or night or wet during the day. They are, of course, ambulant and have no severe behaviour problems.

CAN means continent, ambulant and no severe behaviour disorders. Some may have mild problems.
We sometimes refer briefly to this category as the CANS, and to the more handicapped remainder as the CANTS.

Figures in brackets = numbers receiving formal education or training.

These data raise the question whether, in terms of their capacity, the majority of the children need continuous specialist medical and nursing care either to establish diagnoses or to prevent death, increasing illness or incapacity. Our evidence suggests that nearly all of the intensive diagnostic work is carried out by the paediatricians in paediatric units of general hospitals before children are admitted to the hospitals for the retarded. Moreover, when the children become seriously ill, they are readmitted to paediatric units of general hospitals for diagnosis and specialist medical and nursing care. They remain there until the illness is cured or controlled and are then readmitted to the hospitals for the retarded. The same paediatric services are available to children who live with their families.

A study of McKeown and Leck[9] from Birmingham has also shown the very small proportion of residents of hospitals for the retarded who, at any time, need diagnosis or continuous specialist and nursing care. Moreover, there is no evidence to suggest that the chances of survival or of achieving progress are higher in hospitals for the retarded than at home. Indeed, there is evidence that the progress of moderately retarded children in existing hospitals for the retarded is more limited than among similar children at home.[10–11]

In summary, at the present time in Britain there are roughly 20 children in residential care per 100,000 total population and most of these are in hospitals for the retarded. A further 2 children are on the waiting list for residential care and live, in the meantime, at home. While the majority of children in hospitals have additional severe handicaps of mobility, behaviour and incontinence, the most severely handicapped residents do not appear to be receiving any special formal training and most diagnostic work and intensive medical care is provided outside these institutions by the paediatricians at the general hospitals. The evidence, therefore, suggests that the children in hospitals for the retarded are there only for substitute family care. We will examine later the quality of substitute family care provided in the hospitals.

Adults

Whereas nearly 80% of SSN children live at home with their families, the majority of SSN adults are in hospitals for the mentally retarded. However, the proportion of very severely handicapped adult SSN subjects is much lower than among the children.

Thus, among the 81 SSN adults in institutions per 100,000 total population, no less than 54 (two-thirds) are continent, ambulant and free of severe behaviour disorders. This is because some children with the most severe handicaps will die, and others will progress. In addition, however, more of the very able SSN subjects who have lived all their lives at home will later require residential care when their parents become older, more infirm and ill or die. It might be argued that among adults the ability to walk, continence and the absence of behaviour disorders is too superficial a criterion of ability. However, our data show that of these 54 SSN adults, no less than 39 can *also* feed and wash and dress themselves without any help. Moreover, 21 are rated by their nurses as being of considerable help on the hospital wards or as being usefully employed within the hospitals themselves. The figures in brackets show the proportions receiving formal training. Under one-third of SSN adults in residential care are receiving formal training or education, occupational therapy or work in industrial units. Similarly, under half of the SSN adults at home have these provisions.

Thus, among SSN adults, even more than among the children, the need for continuous specialist medical and nursing care for those in residential care is questioned and the need for substitute home type care is emphasized.

In summary, the total provision for a population of 100,000 is now about 81 places, of which a half are filled by very capable adults who are free of further additional severe handicaps. Moreover, by the time adult status is reached very few SSN subjects with additional severe handicaps are living at home. The waiting list for residential care stands at about 4 per 100,000 total population and the numbers at home with severe handicaps (5) is small in comparison with the number in residential care who have no such handicaps and who can feed and wash and dress themselves without help (39).

There is now an urgent need for the provision in Britain of more residential care for SSN children and adults. The prevalence of SSN adults is rising since survival rates among affected children have improved.[6,7] In addition, there are people waiting for admission to residential care and there is considerable overcrowding in the existing facilities. The existence of the need for more facilities and the pressure to meet the need makes it important that the planning of future provisions takes note of available information on the size and nature of the problem.

An opportunity has thus arisen to evaluate both the effectiveness and the feasibility of different forms of residential care.

There are few people who suggest that future provisions should be developed on precisely the same lines as existing facilities. Indeed, there are many possible ways of providing the new services. If one form of care is to be defended as more effective than another, it should be able to achieve more in the progress of the residents and the relief of problems among the families of handicapped subjects. It should be feasible, both in terms of administration and of costs.

Collaboration between researchers and administrators can result in the provision of services in a manner which is consistent with reasonable experimental designs. Research workers have developed methods of measuring success criteria and administrators are being pressed to provide services.[2] Ethical problems about experimental and control groups do not arise because new facilities cannot be made available to everybody at the same time—people acquiring new services automatically become experimental groups and those who continue to use existing services constitute natural control groups. This type of collaboration is now proceeding in the Wessex Region.

The Regional Hospital Board is to provide new hostel-type hospital units for SSN children and adults, while I and my research colleagues will be observing, both in existing and new facilities, the progress of the residents, the problems of their parents, administrative problems and costs. The detailed proposals are described elsewhere.[4, 5, 18]

Briefly, it is proposed that 275 places, 150 for children and 125 for SSN adults, be provided in the next 10 years. They would be set up in the form of 25-place hostel-type hospital units situated in the main urban centres. Each unit will take in residents from a local catchment area of about 100,000 total population.

During 1970 the Board plans to set up six 25-bed units in areas of 100,000 total population for all of the SSN children who need residential care and whose families live in these areas. A further two 25-bed units are proposed for the more able SSN adults. The first group of units will be evaluated by the research team. The aim of the new facilities is to provide, for populations of 100,000, residential care for those retarded people whose families live within the area. Traditionally, residential care has been provided on a single site for children and adults from much larger total populations, e.g. for a total population of up to a million. The traditional administrative units have therefore been very much larger than those planned in Wessex, and of necessity have been built in relatively isolated areas where sufficient land is available for large complexes of buildings. The new units are small enough to be set up in the centres of urban communities, near the families of the residents and near the leisure, educational, specialist medical and social work facilities available for the community in general and for the retarded who live at home.

It remains to be seen whether these apparent advantages over the traditional form of care produce measurable differences in the children and their families and whether, and at what cost, they can be made to work.

The estimate of numbers and of type of places required for the residential care of the retarded is only one aspect of the problem. Lack of appropriate services places very severe burdens on the families of the retarded who care for them at home, and on the staff of residential institutions. But the problem still arises of the quality of care given in the available facilities.

There is little doubt that the dilemma of whether or not to place a child, normal or retarded, in residential care arises from fear that the quality of care available in institutions will be different, and possibly worse than that within the family home. Early studies showed the retarding effects of institutional care on normal and handicapped children.[13, 17] More intensive studies have revealed the importance of the quality of institutional care as a factor determining the progress of the residents. Professor Tizard showed this in his pioneering study "The Brooklands Experiment".[14]

While it has been possible to describe in general differences in the quality of residential care, only recently have techniques been developed to compare these systematically and reliably.

Professor Tizard and his colleagues Norma Raynes and Roy King have developed and used a scale to describe and to measure the differences in patterns of child care in hospitals, hostels and voluntary homes for SSN children, residential homes and nurseries for deprived children of normal intelligence and hospitals for physically handicapped children also of normal intelligence.[16] They have identified patterns of care which contain very different degrees of the following elements: rigidity, block treatment and regimentation, depersonalization of the children and social distance between children and the child care staff. Management patterns which contain large elements of these qualities have been labelled as "institution oriented" as opposed to the "child oriented" patterns of care which avoid these characteristics.

I will now illustrate the main characteristics of a very "institutionally oriented" pattern of care.

The childrens' day begins when they are all woken up and dressed. The time for waking and dressing is the same every day including Saturdays and Sundays. In institutions where the night staff have to dress the children before the arrival of the day staff at 7.30 a.m., waking and dressing may begin as early as 4.30 a.m., particularly where one child-care staff has 40–60 children to dress. The children then go to the toilets and washrooms together. Here they queue up as they wait for the staff to deal with them. The researchers have described one way of doing this as the "conveyor belt system". One member of the staff undresses the child and places him or her on the toilet; another removes the child and washes the face and hands with a flannel, while a third may brush the child's hair and make final adjustments to the clothing before the child goes out to queue up again, waiting for the time when they will all be told to go to breakfast.

When all have gone through the toilet and washing, the children go to the dining room where they sit around the tables until food arrives. The tables are bare, with the exception of the bowls from which the children eat and one or two implements such as a fork or spoon. The staff serve or feed the children, but do not sit down with them or speak to them. No child rises from the table until all have finished and then all queue up outside the toilet for another session before going to the institution school, to the day-room or out into the play park.

Outside of the schools the staff seldom play with or talk to the children, except to call them to order when conflicts arise.

Morning drinks are handed out to all children at a set time, and lunch, which often starts at 11.30 a.m., is preceded and followed by toiletting procedure. Afternoon activities are similar to those in the morning. The last meal, preceded and followed by toiletting, may be started at 4.00 p.m., and the children are taken to bed as a group, sometimes after bathing, around 5.00 or 6.00 p.m. Children are not read to or sung to, and, unless they are for some reason confined to bed, they are not allowed access to their bedrooms during the day.

The children have no personal effects—i.e. they have no or very few personal books or toys. With the exception of the times when they are visited by their families, they have no personal clothing—they are dressed in clothing collectively available for the unit. These clothes are necessarily often ill-fitting, designed specially for the institution, and are made from fabrics seldom found in ordinary clothing for children.

The institutions investigated showed these phenomena in varying degrees—some showed all and others fewer. However, as a general rule, the hospitals for the retarded tended to show most, residential homes for normal children and local health authority hostels for SSN children showed least, and the remaining types of institution for the retarded such as voluntary homes came midway in this scale. A paediatric hospital for physically handicapped children of normal intelligence was found to be more "institution oriented" than any of the LHA hostels for the retarded, than most voluntary homes for the retarded, and than any residential homes for normal children.

The scale is not particularly sensitive for observing the care of non-ambulant children who cannot, of course, be regimented in this way. Observations made by a working party of the Wessex Regional Hospital Board on units of different kinds throughout the country showed that in "institution oriented" places, non-ambulant children spend long periods of their day on their own, in cots in the dormitory, or sitting up for long periods unattended in chairs around the day-room.[18]

The members of the working party did, however, observe residential units even for the most profoundly handicapped children where these children were involved in play and teaching activities with the other children, where staff ate with the children at tables laid with a cloth and a wide range of crockery and cutlery. The staff spoke and read to the children, took them out in small groups of one or two to the local shops and for walks in the manner characterizing a "child oriented" pattern.

King and Raynes also studied the characteristics of places with different patterns of care.[8] It has been widely believed that size of the administrative unit or of the living unit is an important determinant of management practices. The researchers, however, found that the type of institution and the training of the staff were more important factors than size. Thus, hospital units for the retarded tended to be "institution oriented" regardless of size, while residential units of different sizes for normal children tended to be "child oriented".

Local authority hostels and voluntary homes varied according to staff training more than size. Units with heads trained as nurses tended to be "institution oriented" while those with heads trained in child care or untrained tended to be "child oriented".

Staff training also affected the role the head of the unit played in the day-to-day management of the children, and this in turn affected what went on in the unit. Where heads of units played a substantial part in child care, the unit tended to be "child oriented"—where he or she did mainly administration, the unit tended to be "institution oriented".

King and Raynes have also shown the importance of the role of the junior child care staff.[8] The Wessex Board's working party had earlier undertaken 12-hour studies of the work of the staff in running units of different kinds. In "institution oriented" units we had found it relatively easy to record at quarter-hour intervals the activities of the staff. These tended to be highly routinised, repetitive and specific—for example, child care staff would sort linen or make beds or watch over children for long periods without speaking to or interacting with anyone else. On the other hand, in "child oriented" institutions we found it very difficult to record continuously the activities of child care staff because they were very varied and complex. Thus, a member of staff would be making beds while at the same time speaking to a child who stood near her, and watching another one sitting on a pot. Before making the next bed she would lift the child from the pot and carry him to the sluice room, accompanied by the other child. Having emptied and washed the pot she would return to the bedroom where she dressed the child who had been toiletted. Still chatting to the two children she would return to making beds once again. In their systematic study, King and Raynes showed that this type of role conplexity was associated with "child oriented" care while role specificity and rigidity was found with "institution oriented" care. They also noted that in "child oriented" institutions the child care staff were delegated considerable responsibility for making decisions. Thus, such units were visited by senior administrative staff much less frequently and less formally than "institution oriented" units, which might be visited as often as three times a day, at fixed times, and accompanied by regular written reports. The heads of "child oriented" units were often able to buy their own provisions and children's clothes and toys while "institution oriented units" were serviced from a central kitchen, toys and clothes store.

Nor were the total staffing ratios in the "child oriented" units any higher than in the "institution oriented" ones. The Wessex Board's working party had earler observed that these very different patterns of care could go on with the same total staffing ratios.[8] They observed, however, that there were significant peaks in the working load in the morning when children got up and dressed for breakfast, at midday luch, at teatime and at bedtime. It was our impression that "child oriented" practice was easier if staff were available at *these* times and that at other times staff levels could drop without resulting in "institution oriented" practices. We found that in hospitals for the retarded, staff worked a 12-hour day. This often included a fall in staffing ratios at peak periods because staff didn't eat with the children and some might go off to take their meals when the children had theirs. Similarly, student nurses might go off the ward at peak periods in order to attend lectures. On the other hand in "child oriented" units child care staff worked "split shifts" arranged to cover peak periods, and as they ate with the children they were available at meal times.

Architectural Factors

Very little systematic work has been done in this field. We have seen "institution oriented" practices in reasonably well-designed buildings, and "child oriented" practices in buildings designed for every purpose other than child care. Before closing, I would, however, like to mention very briefly some architectural features of buildings which seem to have a profound influence on the management patterns of institutions.

The first of these is day-room space. The Ministry of Health standards for overcrowding are concerned largely with bedroom space, although it can be argued that while space around the bed is important, for most of the time beds are occupied their incumbents are unconscious. It is quite usual to find even newly built hospitals or hostel units with one day-room for the residents.

The effect of this, particularly in "institution oriented" units which disallow residents open access to their bedrooms or dormitories during the day, is that a single day-room may contain between 20 and 60 residents simultaneously.

The quality of social relationships possible under these circumstances is then very limited. Indeed, there cannot be many situations where between 2 and 5 football or hockey teams are encouraged to spend large periods of the day in one room. This problem is compounded in units where the day-room and dining room accommodation is shared. For those periods of the day when the tables are being set for meals, and until they have been cleared, substantial areas of the day-room cannot be used at all. A number of day-rooms enable the residents to form smaller social groups, to communicate very much less noisily and more intensively, and to undertake different activities at the same time. Childrens' hostels now being designed in the Wessex Region for 25 children will have at least three day-rooms in addition to the dining room, and children will also have access to their bedrooms when they wish to go there.

The second outstanding feature we have noticed is the lack of accessibility of toilets to residents, even in recently designed units. Residents spend most of the day in the day-room or the playground attached to the unit. It is not unusual, particularly if any of the residents tend to be overactive and to wander, to lock the door of the room the residents are in, or to lock the entrance to the unit when they are in the playgrounds. One of the commonest problems among the SSN child or adult is that of incontinence and it is clearly in the interest of both resident and staff that the resident should learn to be continent and use a lavatory on his or her own. In many existing buildings, a resident who wishes to go to the lavatory must first attract the attention of a member of staff and communicate his needs. The staff member has then to take out his keys and unlock the door of the day-room in order to let the resident have access to the lavatory. It is not uncommon, in our experience, for the staff member to have to unlock two doors—one between the playground and the day-room and a second between the day-room and the corridor separating the day-room from the lavatory. I can think of no way of encouraging incontinence more effectively than this among people with learning problems and without speech. Lavatories accessible to the day-room from within and to the playground from without are, I believe, essential. Outside lavatories would also make for a more effective programme of care.

A third problem is accessibility of drinking water. Other than the taps in the toilets or bathroom, there may be no other access for the residents of an "institution oriented" unit where the kitchen and scullery are out of bounds to most residents. Residents are faced with the problem just mentioned of communicating their thirst to staff members or getting something to drink. It seems, *a priori*, that it must be very difficult for non-speaking residents to do this; one can only speculate on how often thirst goes unrecognized or results in difficult behaviour. I have, however, seen the various strategies resorted to by thirsty patients without access to taps. Water fountains available both in the day-rooms and in the playground would probably overcome the problem among all but the most profoundly or physically handicapped residents.

Conclusions

Important conclusions emerge from these studies. First, the pattern of care in any institution for residential care does not depend solely on its size, staffing ratio, the handicaps of its residents or the degree of dedication of its staff. Second, "institution oriented" practices are not necessarily "convenient" to child-care staff or efficient for administration. Indeed, they may often be both inconvenient and inefficient.

Much further research will be required to understand the complex factors which are involved. It seems clear, however, that if we wish new units to be "child oriented", highly specific administrative aims must be drawn up to avoid "institution oriented" practices and staff training at all levels must include "child oriented" practices as their main aim.

I am also more optimistic now that, if we so desire, "child oriented" practices can be introduced in units where "institution oriented" care now prevails. I believe that the first step in this direction will require not only a commitment to "child orientation" by the personnel in positions of authority in these institutions; they will need to define specifically, and in detail, which of the components of "institution orientation" they plan to avoid and which of the features of "child orientation" they aim to implement.

Having done this, the task of implementing these can be worked out by all levels of staff concerned. Moreover, continual assessment can be made of the extent to which the aims are being achieved and the obstacles analysed, removed or bypassed.

The problem of innovating large, complex organizations is not to be underestimated, but there are many historical examples that such changes do occur.[1] The management skills for effecting such changes are just as necessary in institutions for the retarded as in complex industrial and commercial organizations.

In commerce and industry these skills are being recognized and taught. They might yet be usefully directed in the services of the retarded.

It is, perhaps, paradoxical that innovating techniques of management skills applied in industrial organizations seem now to offer possibilities for humanizing residential care of the handicapped.

We are now only beginning to understand the key problems of providing residential care for SSN subjects in sufficient numbers and of high quality. The information available and the need to provide further facilities offers new opportunities to both researchers and service personnel to measure how well the aims of the service are being met.

It is hoped that these opportunities will be taken and that they will produce both better services and a greater understanding of retardation itself.

At present parents of SSN children and administrators tend to see residential care as a permanent and separate alternative to care of the child at home. The need for residential care is seen to arise when the parents can no longer cope. As residential care of high quality becomes more easily accessible to parents, I believe that it will be made available much earlier than now and for short periods. This would aim to relieve the families of their burdens at regular intervals and allow them opportunities for leisure activities which would, in turn, protect their health and their ability to fulfil all of their social obligations, including that of caring for the handicapped child. If these periods of care were to be regular and available in a local hostel familiar to both child and parent, it could be an experience which would both add to the child's own resources and prepare child and family for the day when permanent residential care becomes inevitable.

These ideas, and others, remain to be tested. In the meantime, one thing is clear. We will not know the true potential of the severely mentally retarded until we have begun to provide them with the effective services they need. We have a long way to go.

References

1. Burns, T. and Stalker, G. M. *The Management of Innovation*. Tavistock Publications, 1961.

2. GRAD, J. and SAINSBURY, P. Evaluating the community psychiatric service in Chichester: results. *Milbank Mem. Fd. Quart.* 1966, **44** (i), Suppl. 246–78.
3. KING, R. D. and RAYNES, N. V. Patterns of institutional care for the severely subnormal. *Amer. J. Ment. Defic.* 1968, **72,** 700–9.
4. KUSHLICK, A. A method of evaluating the effectiveness of a Community Health Service. *Soc. Econ. Admin.* 1967, **1,** 29–48.
5. KUSHLICK, A. The Wessex Experiment—comprehensive care for the mentally subnormal. *Brit. Hosp. J. Soc. Serv. Rev.* 6 Oct. 1967.
6. KUSHLICK, A. and COX, R. The ascertained prevalence of mental subnormality in the Wessex Region on 1st July 1963. *Proc. 1st Cong. Int. Ass. Sci. Stud. Ment. Defic.*, Montpellier, 1967.
7. KUSHLICK, A. and COX, G. R. Wessex Regional Hospital, 1969.
8. KING, R. D. and RAYNES, N. V. An operational measure of inmate management in residential institutions. *Soc. Sci. Med.* 1968, **2,** 41–53.
9. LECK, I., GORDON, W. L. and MCKEOWN, T. Medical and social needs of patients in hospitals for the mentally subnormal. *Brit. J. Prev. Soc. Med.* 1967, **21,** 115–21.
10. LYLE, J. G. The effect of an institution environment upon the verbal development of imbecile children. I: Verbal intelligences. *J. Ment. Defic. Res.* 1959, **3,** 122–8; II: Speech and language. *J. Ment. Defic. Res.* 1960, **4,** 1–13; III: The Brooklands Residential Family Unit. *J. Ment. Defic. Res.* 1960, **4,** 14–23.
11. LYLE, J. G. Some factors affecting the speech development of imbecile children in an institution. *J. Child Psychol. Psychiat.* 1960, **1,** 121–9.
12. RAYNES, N. V. and KING, R. D. The measurement of child management in residential institutions for the retarded. *Proc. 1st Cong. Int. Ass. Sci. Stud. Ment. Defic.*, Montpellier, 1967.
13. SPITZ, R. A. Hospitalism: an inquiry into the genisis of psychiatric conditions in early childhood. *Psychoanal. Stud. Child.* 1945, **1,** 53–74.
14. TIZARD, J. Residential care of mentally handicapped children. *Brit. Med. J.* 1960, **1,** 1041–6.
15. TIZARD, J. and GRAD, J. C. *The Mentally Handicapped and Their Families. A Social Survey*, (Maudsley Monograph No. 7), London, Oxford University Press, 1961.
16. TIZARD, J., KING, R. D., RAYNES, N. V. and YULE, W. The care and treatment of subnormal children in residential institutions. *Proc. 1st Int. Conf. Ass. Spec. Educ.*, Eltham, London, 1966.
17. BOWLBY, J. *Maternal Care and Mental Health.* Geneva, World Health Organization, 1952.
18. WESSEX REGIONAL HOSPITAL BOARD. Provision of future accommodation for the mentally subnormal. Report of a Working Party. Winchester, Wessex Regional Hospital Board, 1966.

Paper No. 2

ELSPETH STEPHEN, MA, DIPED
Principal Psychologist, Queen Mary's Hospital for Children, Carshalton

and

JEAN ROBERTSON, BSC, DIPPSYCH
Senior Psychologist, Queen Mary's Hospital for Children, Carshalton

IN this paper we would like to talk about the residential care of low-grade severely subnormal children. By low-grade severely subnormal children we mean idiots and borderline idiot/imbeciles. We define, in terms of I.Q., idiots as children with I.Q.s of less than 20 and idiot/imbeciles as children with I.Q.s of about 20. In terms of mental age the idiot children we are going to discuss had mental ages of 12–15 months or less and the idiot/imbeciles had mental ages of about 18 months–2 years.

It seems to us useful to describe our experience of the behaviour of these children for three reasons. First, their care presents problems which we think are different from the problems arising in the care of trainable imbecile children with I.Q.s of 20–50. Second, these children may well make up a significant percentage of severely subnormal children requiring residential care. In our hospital of 340 long-term patients, all of whom are children, 24% are clearly in the imbecile range, 11% are in the borderline idiot/imbecile range and 65% are idiots. Primrose,[(2)] in a recent article in *Devol. Med. & Child Neurol.* gives some support to our findings. He reports a survey of children in the Mental Deficiency Hospitals of Glasgow and Argyll. This survey was carried out on 1st January 1967. Of 269 children, 253 were severely subnormal (I.Q. less than 50) of whom 60%

were idiots. From this it seems to us that although our hospital population may not be representative of all the children in Mental Deficiency hospitals in terms of grade of severity of mental handicap, it does suggest that these low-grade children constitute quite a large group of children in Mental Deficiency hospitals and therefore should be studied. Third, we were unable to find any description of the management of these children. In fact, Dr. Woodward[(4)] at the Fountain Hospital seems to be one of the few people who has concerned herself with the behaviour of idiots.

Our experience of these children occurred in the course of an experiment which we carried out in one of our hospital wards from 1964 to 1967. The aim of this experiment was to see whether we could adapt the 'Brooklands' findings[(3)] to a hospital ward and also whether low-grade severely subnormal children as well as imbecile children would respond to such a régime. There were 20 children in the ward: of these 20, 9 children (45%) were clearly of imbecile level, 5 (25%) were of borderline idiot/imbecile level and 6 (30%) were idiots. They ranged in age from 2 to 10 years in 1964. The children in the Experimental Ward were matched on Chronological Age and I.Q. with a group of children in other wards of the hospital and mongols were matched with mongols. At the beginning and end of the experiment the children in both groups were assessed on scales of self-help, speech and language, verbal and non-verbal ability. Throughout the experiment observations were made of their social development and level of play. The low-grade children did not differ from the brighter children in terms of age, length of time in hospital or number of adverse home factors.

The régime on the Ward was based on that of a residential Nursery as far as possible. On the Ward the children were divided into two family groups and great emphasis was laid on an individual approach to each child, on fostering relationships between staff and children and between child and child, on supplying appropriate play equipment, creating opportunities for play and in giving the children as much experience of the outside world as we could through frequent visits to private homes, shops, etc. The imbecile children went to a class run on Nursery School lines and some of the idiot/imbecile children also went to this class half-time. The idiot children remained on the Ward while the others were at school.

We think it is important to remember when considering the care of severely subnormal children that the major part of their time is spent at home or, in our case, in the Ward. This meant that the 20 children spent most of their time together—the family groups each containing a cross-section of all the children in terms of grade of handicap.

We will now describe the behaviour of the low-grade children, the idiots and borderline idiot/imbecile children. Their behaviour changed hardly at all during the $3\frac{1}{2}$ years of the experiment.

First the idiot/imbecile children. This is a description of their behaviour in the nursery class. "The children with I.Q.s around 20 presented many problems; not only was it difficult to get them to settle, but they disrupted the activities of the rest of the group. Both their use and comprehension of speech was limited, they only used the equipment if they were given individual help, and their attention span was short. They were fond of throwing and tipping up furniture and equipment and were sometimes aggressive towards the other children." Their behaviour on the Ward was much the same. They were dependent on adults; alone with an adult they might copy her activities in a simple manner, e.g. folding clothes, tidying up, and some of their aggressive behaviour towards other children seemed to be due to jealousy of adults' attention. In fact, in their dependence on adults, their aggression to other children and exploratory destructive play and in other ways they resembled normal toddlers. However, their relative size and strength, and above all their apparent inability to outgrow this stage, made this behaviour a major problem.

The children in the idiot range had a Mental Age of approximately 9–12 months. In many respects they did not resemble normal children of this age. Many of them showed no response to adults beyond watching them or taking toys offered by them. They did not smile or show that they enjoyed attention. Much of their vocalization consisted of shrieking or singing noises; sounds were not often used in an attempt to communicate. They did not show a great interest in toys and some children simply incorporated toys into their manneristic movements. These children presented no behaviour problems, but they were a nursing problem as they needed total care.

During school hours when the low-grade children were alone in the Ward we drew up a programme for each child which the nursing staff carried out. This was called "the Play Programme", but in fact it involved walking and speech as well as play. This programme was based on observation of the children by a psychologist and nurses plus a knowledge of the stage each child had reached on Piaget's scale of sensori-motor intellectual development[4] and on an "Ad Hoc" Speech Scale. For the play equipment provided for this Group we were indebted to the suggestions of Mrs. Goldschmied with her experience of normal pre-Nursery school children.

The most heavily handicapped children were encouraged to feel different textures, to listen to varying sounds while the adult talked to them at "mother distance". The most intelligent, i.e. the borderline idiot/imbeciles, were encouraged to build, to explore size and shape, simple speech was used with them and they were encouraged to name one or two objects and to co-operate with other children and the adult in play. This programme was revised about once a year with the help of the nursing staff, but essentially revision varied in content but not in complexity or level of play, speech or personal relationships.

One of the advantages of this programme was that every child was played with. It is only too easy to ignore the quiet low-grade child because of the demands of the active children. In fact, although at first the children played in their own family room, we soon found it better to divide the group in terms of grade of handicap as the active children in each group demanded all the adults' attention.

Formal results on scales of verbal, non-verbal ability and self-help. Results on these scales confirmed the finding that while the imbecile children responded to the régime of the Experimental Ward, the low-grade children did not change on the whole.

At the end of the experiment the imbecile children showed more improvement than the children in the control group on all the scales.

The idiot/imbeciles showed a little progress in self-help skills and more progress than the controls.

The idiot children showed no change on any scale.

The total group of low-grade children made slightly more progress than the control group in verbal and non-verbal ability, but the most striking feature was the limited amount of change that took place; some children did not make any progress and even seemed to do less than they were doing at the beginning. This tendency to do less was more marked in the control group than in the experimental group.

As a further assessment information was collected describing the children's responsiveness to people and their general adjustment. The children were seen individually in the company of people they knew and the nursing staff were asked for a variety of information on their day-to-day behaviour. There was little difference between the two groups of low-grade children in their responsiveness to adults and response to speech, but there was evidence that the low-grade experimental children were better on measures of general and emotional adjustment, they showed less aggressive behaviour and had fewer tempers and attacks of screaming than the children in the control group.

We think that the borderline idiot/imbecile group did not respond to our régime. They seemed to need a more structured and secure environment, with less freedom of choice of activities. Their progress was so slow and the difficult behaviour went on for so long that it did impose a strain on the children themselves, the other children and on the staff.

Julie is an extreme example of the idiot/imbecile child. She was hyperkinetic, destructive and inaccessible. At one of the weekly Ward meetings one year after the start of the experiment, Julie's progress was discussed. The yearly assessment showed that she had made a little progress on two scales of self-help but in nothing else. Julie's uncontrollable behaviour had made it virtually impossible to carry out the play programme on the Ward because she had to be watched over all the time. Sister said that she would attempt to do things, such as putting bricks into a container, but lost concentration after a few seconds. She had good days when she was quite tranquil, but on other days she was not only a danger to herself but to other children. So far she had not hurt other children seriously because she was watched over all the time. The Consultant said that Julie presented a severe nursing problem and that the only answer seemed to be constant adult supervision.

The idiot/imbecile children needed a lot of help in self-care and because of their behaviour tended to disrupt the group and made great demands on the staff out of proportion to their number and responsiveness and to the detriment of the other children. We have not found the answer to the problem of the management of this group of children. It may be that they would respond to a carefully worked out programme of behaviour modification.

The group of idiot children, on the other hand, did not present behaviour or management problems, but as they remained totally helpless, except that 4 could walk, they needed total care. These helpless idiot children could be cared for with the imbecile children, some of whom mothered the helpless children.

Although the idiot children showed little improvement in behaviour, it may be that they were less disturbed than they had been. We think the care of this group of children raises problems of job satisfaction.

We would like to end with a quotation. G. Dybward[1] in a paper given at the Montpellier Conference on the Scientific Study of Mental Deficiency writes: "While for the vast majority of those in mental retardation institutions a stimulating environment is the greatest need, there are some individuals with cerebral damage for whom our present state of knowledge suggests that the extent of their external stimulation must be curtailed and an environment created which is limiting and re-assuring."

We would like to thank all the staff on the Ward for their co-operation in caring for these children.

References

1. DYBWARD, G. Changing patterns of residential care for the mentally retarded. A challenge to architecture. *Proc. 1st Cong. Int. Ass. Sci. Stud. Ment. Defic.*, Montpellier, 1967.
2. PRIMROSE, D. A. A. Children in the mental deficiency hospitals of Glasgow and Argyll. *Develop. Med. Child Neurol.* 1968, **10,** 366–73.
3. TIZARD, J. *The Brooklands Residential Unit*, pp. 85–137, Pt. IV: in *Community Services for the Mentally Handicapped*. London, Oxford University Press, 1964.
4. WOODWARD, M. The behaviour of idiots interpreted by Piaget's theory of sensori-motor development. *Brit. J. Educ. Psychol.* 1959, **29,** 60–71.

Paper No. 3

M. E. York-Moore, MB, BS, DPM

Consultant Psychiatrist, South Ockendon Hospital, and Essex County Council Mental Health Service

The organizers of this Symposium are to be congratulated on their choice of subject; it is a large, patchy and challenging field in which to roam. My brief is to present to you some purely personal observations on the present state of residential care as I find it in practice, bearing in mind that my work involves me in both the hospital and local health authority domains.

May we take certain things for granted, in the interests of time? Firstly, my remarks apply almost entirely to the severely subnormal; then I would like you to accept that I strongly favour small residential units, though these may, or may not, be part of a much larger establishment; reasonable privacy for each handicapped person; and the possession of personal clothing and articles like photographs, ornaments, pictures and toys. Whilst many who are in residential care are dressed in a normal fashion for their age, with the liberal use of bright colours and attention to a reasonable fit, I can see no valid reason why this should not apply to everyone.

I must also ask you to take for granted that I strongly believe in the importance of individual and small group training methods in the management of the severely subnormal person, however disturbed his behaviour or severe his physical handicaps may be.

I attach great importance to studies of the kind we have heard about this evening, and of the kind recently undertaken by Dr. Pauline Morris (and due to be published soon) and Raynes and King published earlier this year.[2-4] These studies are often capable of acting as the catalyst which sets off a re-orientation process in which the dynamics of an aspect of residential care is better understood and can therefore be more effectively developed at grass-root level. They also point the way for those who pace the corridors of power and upon whose deliberations and decisions we are, in the final analysis, so dependent to make the progress we wish.

I am going to concentrate on here-and-now aspects and will limit my remarks about the future to some humble suggestions for the immediate or near future, believing with a deep, unshakeable conviction—and I would be so glad to be proved wrong on this—that anything requiring large financial or staffing resources, when applied on a widespread, national basis, is likely to be projected so far into the future as to bear little or no relevance to solving the many serious problems which exist now.

There are now in England and Wales some 55 local health authority hostels accommodating 1031 mentally subnormal children, 110 hostels for 2328 adults and 4 hostels for a mixed population of 65 mentally ill and mentally subnormal people. I have been impressed from my own experience by the bias towards individualization and self-dependence that hostel residents enjoy. No doubt the finding of Raynes and King (when they made a comparative study of hostel and hospital care recently) that there was a striking similarity between the role performance (as measured by verbal contact) of heads of units and patterns of management when looked at from the point of view of training is one important explanation of this bias. Other factors which I suggest have a bearing on this are the attitudes of all the staff and the freedom from old legacies handed down from the past (for example overcrowding and unsuitable old buildings). It would be interesting to make a comparative study along similar lines in long-established and newly-built hospitals.

Hostel care for children has qualities about it which are different to that for adults. There tends to be a higher turn-over of residents and as many children can spend weekends and training centre holidays at home, it is possible to accommodate an appreciable number of short-term care cases during these times. The Essex County Council children's hostel, which has been open 6 years, accommodates 22 children. There have been, during the first 5 years, a total of 126 admissions of which 68 were short-term and

58 long-term, and there were over twice the number of boys than girls. The Warden has found it essential to keep a link with the homes of all the children for, without quite elaborate arrangements made by him, these links easily become tenuous and broken. One interesting scheme to encourage parents to keep in touch with their child is an arrangement whereby parents can phone the hostel early in the evening to speak to their child, and often, of course, they have a word with the Warden at the same time.

I am doubtful whether it is best to mix too wide an age range in a children's hostel; a number of the older boys, and to a less though still significant extent older girls, have become domineering and sometimes quite aggressive towards the younger children. I think one ought to try and group the children by behaviour and physical maturity rather than by any chronological yard-stick. If there is more than one hostel to serve an area, then obviously a more effective segregation of cases becomes possible. This has to be balanced, however, against the desirability of having hostels reasonably near the children's own homes and maintaining a family structure within the hostel.

There is not the time to give other examples, but I have found that an imaginative Warden—or Houseparent, which is probably a better term—can, if given freedom to develop his ideas, introduce new techniques which are often the result of a previous experiment in training, and almost always these seem to emerge through play, rather than formal teaching situations.

Therefore, the children's hostel is an ever-changing picture, with children leaving as they grow older and younger ones replacing them. The adult hostel I have found to be quite different. A great deal depends on the type of resident primarily catered for; if most of them are severely subnormal with few, if any, links with their own homes, the tendency is towards a fairly static hostel population, vacancies occurring only very occasionally and usually singly. This makes it very difficult to transfer suitable hospital patients to hostels in groups, apart from the lucky ones who may be transferred when a hostel first opens. This problem of the single transfer is a very real one. I recently had experience of trying three hospital patients who were regarded as very suitable for hostel care, before

I managed to get one of them to settle in the hostel. If I had been able to transfer all three together I would think it possible that they would have all settled. The two who did not settle insisted—in no uncertain fashion I should add—on returning to hospital in spite of much tactful persuasion by the Warden and others, including myself, to give the hostel a longer trial. One must remember that severely subnormal adults have the same freedom to stay or go as anyone else—persuasion is all we have to use and, I hasten to add, a good thing too.

When the turn-over of cases in an Essex County Council 30-bedded hostel for severely subnormal women which has been open five years was recently studied, I found that there had been 49 admissions, including 4 re-admissions, and a small number of short-term care cases. Residents tend not to have long holidays at home; some have no homes. Thus it means that holiday vacancies occur for short-term cases relatively infrequently.

Campbell,[1] in a survey of 14 hostels for mentally disordered adults in Lancashire, regarded them as functioning primarily as long-term homes; she found that 8% of the 355 subnormal and severely subnormal residents had returned to the community, and 12% of the subnormal and severely subnormal group had been discharged from the hostels to hospital. Comparative figures for the Essex women's hostel I have just mentioned indicate that 27% of the total admissions have returned to the community (both samples having a majority returning to their own homes), and 10% have been transferred to subnormality hospitals. When the numbers of hostel admissions which were from subnormality hospitals are compared in both groups, 42% were found in Campbell's sample and 45% in the Essex sample. Thus although the two hostel samples are made up with similar proportions of residents admitted from hospital, and the two samples discharged similar proportions to hospitals, the Essex sample discharged a significantly larger proportion (beyond the 0·001 level) to the community.

The reasons for this difference are not clear; they could lie in a difference in the type of resident admitted to hostels in the two samples (some factor other than admission from hospital) or they could lie in the nature of the hostel care. What is important is that both samples indicate the practical possibility of hostels functioning to some extent as part of an on-going rehabilitative process.

Attention to the selection of residents is important if the best use is to be made of the scarce places available in hostels; it helps to have a multi-disciplinary selection team, with the Warden having the power to say "No" to a referral if he feels he cannot cope. It also helps, in my opinion, to have a very flexible trial period system. For example, to exclude a child from hostel care because he is incontinent may remove the one chance the child has of overcoming his incontinence—a short trial period will show whether or not hostel care, with its particular training influences, will help that child. For this reason I do not go along with the idea that local authority hostels should not have facilities, like sluices, to be able to provide this kind of service. The same principle holds good for behaviour disorders, for unless there is a degree of tolerance towards and understanding about these things amongst staff and management, the hostel will not serve its community as fully and effectively as it should.

A warmly empathetic, psychiatrically-orientated staff attitude is the one most likely to survive, in my view, after many a trying problem of the kind I have mentioned. I have found that it is much more a question of the personality of individual staff than any one type of training, which shows up those who are cut-out for this kind of residential work. I hope I need hardly add that for any hostel worker appropriate training is essential, in order that the best service can be provided and also that there is some reasonably attractive career structure surrounding the work.

A final point about hostels—it is important to remember that just because there is a small residential unit for severely subnormal children, or adults, in the middle of a housing estate, there is no automatic guarantee that the isolation factor associated with hospitalization will disappear. Hostels can be islets in the community, and a good deal of thought and effort, especially by the Warden, is needed to combat this.

Moving now to a consideration of the hospital aspects of residential care, there seem to me to be certain basic problems at the present time, even though there are variations between hospitals in terms of staff attitudes, proportion of subnormal to severely subnormal patients, the existence, or not, of legacies from the past, and so forth. Society has inherited a form of hospital care for the subnormal which stems from traditional general hospital management methods, and which has to cope with a very formidable burden in terms of care. It has, of course, a limited priority financially, though society is generally sympathetic to those who are handicapped and those who work with the handicapped. However, there is a combination of factors which tend to make it all too easy for the needs of the subnormal, particularly the hospitalized subnormal, to be overlooked. The first basic problem is therefore one of lack of public awareness and concern. The efforts of the National Society for Mentally Handicapped Children to combat this needs no reminder from me here tonight.

The next basic problem which besets many hospitals is overcrowding. I regard overcrowding as the most pernicious force in our hospital service. It is hard to exaggerate the damage it causes: it obviously makes privacy very difficult to achieve; personal possessions are a liability rather than an asset; inter-personal difficulties are greater for both patients and staff, and tensions are likely to build up, producing an anti-therapeutic environment. Subnormality nursing has never been a wildly attractive job; overcrowding, working in its insidious way, coupled with large wards, are potent deterrents to work satisfaction.

The third basic problem, which is linked with the previous two, is staff shortage and staff recruitment. This problem varies to some extent in different parts of the country, and is, I believe, influenced by the local employment situation as well as the reputation and efforts of the hospitals individually. Nurse recruitment in many areas is dependent to a greater or lesser degree on applicants from overseas, without whom I believe the service in these areas at the present time would succumb. The difficulties that some nurses face in their hour-by-hour care of patients in overcrowded wards are very great indeed. One has to be really close to the situation to appreciate just how much "vocational effort" is expected of nurses at times, and there is a danger that it can be taken just a little bit too much for granted. I believe we have a duty to try to make the job of caring for hospitalized patients more satisfying and to ensure that unreasonable demands on personal skills and the physical and mental reserves of staff are not made. If I have appeared to thrice underline the importance of considering the future role of the subnormality nurse I will have achieved my purpose. To me it is unrealistic and unwise to plan for the residential care of severely subnormal people without taking very careful account of the need to devise, positively and constructively, ways of building up the nursing service which now exists. I will mention some ways of doing this later.

So I come to the last part of my paper—some suggestions for short-term developments which, I hope, gain in realism what they may lack in originality or cloud-cuckoo optimism. Firstly to make hostel work as attractive as possible, appropriate training and a reasonable career structure are essential.

Next, we are not going to witness a large-scale movement of patients from hospital into the community, partly because there is only a limited amount of accommodation available in the community, and partly because it is quite conjectural how many of those in-patients, who are regarded as suitable for hostel care, will prove to be so in practice. Campbell,[1] for example, found in her Lancashire census that 58 of the 273 hostel residents (21%) who were admitted from hospital returned to hospital, and in the Essex study 5 out of 22 (23%) returned to hospital. Transfer of patients calls for careful preparation, group transfers whenever possible, and a flexible, well-integrated policy of both hospital and local authority. What is really needed in practice is a continuum of care, so that as the handicapped person's needs change, so can the type of care.

The need to improve standards in hospitals is very pressing; every opportunity should be taken to reduce overcrowding; and such action should be backed by an official policy revising minimum standards for sleeping and living accommodation in *existing* buildings and special attention should be given to the division of large wards into small units. The effect on staff of 50 beds becoming two 25-bedded units can be dramatic. Public awareness of the problems surrounding the care of the subnormal could be increased. I prefer the non-sensational, realistic kind of fact-giving information via the usual media.

Tizard[5] states that: "it is the social organisation of our present residential institutions for the retarded which is the main factor responsible for the poor quality of care which many of them provide". To change the social organization is no easy task, but a beginning might well be made by revising the work of the subnormality nurse at all levels. With the more heavily handicapped or behaviour-disturbed type of patient now accumulating in our subnormality hospitals, whilst the less handicapped is increasingly cared for in the community, it seems to me we need to weave together staff possessing nursing skills and staff trained in child care. I think it would be unwise, and even dangerous, to separate these two disciplines. Certainly a re-orientation of nurse training towards child care principles, the use of training and education methods in the day-to-day management of patients, and the integration of a fostering with a sick-nursing role is needed, but it is really a case of enriching existing skills, not of replacing them. With regard to improving recruitment of nurses, surely some national scheme could be devised immediately, whereby localities which have a surplus of applicants could aid those which are short of staff—a kind of national employment bureau. The entry of staff with a child-care orientated background into hospital work is to be welcomed and expedited, providing such staff will fully accept the awkward hours of work which residential care demands and providing they can be spliced into, rather than replace, a re-orientated nursing structure with an altered social organization.

The last basic problem I shall mention is the waiting list one. As far as hostels are concerned I see little point in keeping anything more than a short waiting list, as most cases arise from a threatened or actual crisis in the home. In such circumstances, those who cannot be admitted have to be found accommodation elsewhere: a private home or hospital, usually.

The position of the hospital waiting lists reminds me of a log-jam. Lists are often very long and contain many urgent problems, and they do not usually allow for the cases which arise suddenly and unexpectedly in the community, which either need hospital care or cannot be found hostel-type residential care elsewhere. This hidden case-load tends to cut across any workable scheme for the allocation of priorities on the waiting list. It is very difficult to admit cases as their needs dictate because of overcrowding. The situation is worse, it seems, in some parts of the country than in others—perhaps use could be made of any vacant accommodation (if it exists) on a national rather than regional basis. Apart from this suggestion, we surely need more residential accommodation urgently, principally hostel in type, but this *must* be coupled with the appropriate adaptation of existing hospital wards to make them usable for the more handicapped type of case. This is really a most important point.

Finally, we can continue to work towards an increasingly integrated effort from the several disciplines involved in residential care. We can all afford to listen to and learn from our colleagues in other disciplines; sometimes we receive support from them, sometimes we can give it; the main thing is that channels of communication are opened up through all strata of staff—and kept that way.

Experimentation in forms of care must go on, but to quote Tizard again, who said of the studies of Raynes and King: "these conclusions are, however, tentative, and it would be irresponsible, on the basis of limited survey data alone, to advocate wholesale changes in our residential services for the retarded—even if such changes were feasible in the near future. Except in times of crisis, surveys of existing practice should be followed by experiment before radical changes in social policy are introduced on a wide scale." This seems to me to be eminently sensible advice, providing that in our pre-occupation with "what might be" we do not fail to attend *realistically* to the urgent improvements needed to "what we already have". It seems clear to me that on a national scale we are governed in what we achieve in the foreseeable future by what limited funds are made available for developments and—what is to my mind more important—the imaginative use of what resources we have available to us.

References

1. Campbell, A. Characteristics of 352 residents and 119 ex-residents of 14 Lancashire County Council hostels for mentally disordered adults. *Med. Offr.* 1968, **119,** 3–6.
2. Rayne, N. V. and King, R. D. The measurement of child management in residential institutions for the retarded. *Proc. 1st Cong. Int. Ass. Sci. Stud. Ment. Defic.*, Montpellier, 1967.
3. King, R. D. and Raynes, N. V. Some determinants of patterns of residential care. *Proc. 1st Cong. Int. Ass. Sci. Stud. Ment. Defic.*, Montpellier, 1967.

4. King, R. D. and Raynes, N. V. Patterns of institutional care for the severely subnormal. *Amer. J. Ment. Defic.* 1968, **72,** 700–9.
5. Tizard, J. Residential care for the mentally retarded. *Proc. 1st Cong. Int. Ass. Sci. Stud. Ment. Defic.*, Montpellier, 1967.

Participants in the Discussion

B. H. KIRMAN, MD, DPM (*Chairman*)
Consultant Psychiatrist, Fountain and Carshalton Hospital Group; Hon. Associate Physician, St. George's and Maudsley Hospitals; Chairman, Research Committee, IRMR.

MILDRED CREAK, MD, FRCP, DPM
Formerly Consultant Psychiatrist, Hospital for Sick Children, London.

G. DUTTON, MD
Physician Superintendent and Consultant Psychiatrist, South Ockendon Hospital Group; Consultant Psychiatrist, John F. Kennedy Centre, Newham.

V. GORMAN, SRN, RHMS
Principal Nursing Officer, Northgate and District Hospital, Morpeth, Northumberland.

A. KUSHLICK, MB, BCH, MRCP, DPH
Director of Research into Subnormality, Wessex Regional Hospital Board.

JEAN ROBERTSON, BSC, DIPPSYCH
Senior Psychologist, Queen Mary's Hospital for Children, Carshalton.

ELSPETH STEPHEN, MA, DIPED
Principal Psychologist, Queen Mary's Hospital for Children, Carshalton.

M. E. YORK-MOORE, MB, BS, DPM
Consultant Psychiatrist, South Ockendon Hospital and Essex County Council Mental Health Service.

Discussion and Chairman's Summary

CREAK: Asked whether the comparative lack of response shown by the low-grade children might be accounted for by the fact that they had spent more time in Hospital than the more responsive children.

STEPHEN: Stated that she and Miss Robertson had considered this and there seemed to be no difference between the responsive and unresponsive groups either in terms of length of time in Hospital, age, or on age of admission or number of adverse home conditions.

DUTTON: Queried the applicability of Dr. Kushlick's prevalence figures to his area.

KUSHLICK: Stated that the gross prevalence rates might not apply to a particular area. It might be necessary to look at specific rates, such as age-specific rates.

DUTTON: Stated that the introduction of split shifts, as suggested by Dr. Kushlick, was not practicable as this was not approved by the General Nursing Council.

GORMAN: Stated that the needs of the nursing of the Mentally Subnormal wanted reviewing, particularly Nurse Training. He thought that the emphasis in training should be geared to child care, house Father–Mother training, social work with some aspects of education, as against the present emphasis on medical care and various syndromes. He had asked the Institute if they could undertake such a review. He felt that Nurses are not necessarily the best people to review their own work, although it would be necessary for Nurses to form a part of any working party reviewing the situation. Secondly, reorganization of the working staff during the day so that they could work with patients in places such as Industrial Units would obviate the need to bring in staff during the morning or late in the evening to give adequate cover. Bringing in part-time staff for a few hours in the morning and again in the evening would present a tremendous problem.

Chairman's Summary

It is now much more than a century since the founding of the early idiot asylums at Colchester, Earlswood, in Switzerland, Germany and elsewhere. At different times those responsible for such ventures hoped that they would provide something of a self-contained colony where all the inhabitants would live happily on Utopian,

Owenite lines. They were to provide a refuge from the ills of society after the industrial revolution and at a time when other social provision was lacking.

The contributions to this symposium provide well-documented evidence of how far short Institutions for the mentally handicapped have fallen of the aims of their founders. The rapid development of social services and the metamorphosis of society provide a setting in which the mentally retarded can be accepted and habilitated as far as possible as an integral part of the general community. In this situation the existing hospitals are archaic structurally and more particularly in their social structure.

The speakers have indicated how, on the basis of careful survey and scientific study, a change can be effected in the direction of small residential substitute homes for those of the mentally handicapped who cannot live in their own homes. Developments on these lines may do much to relieve the problems of overcrowding and ill-adapted régimes which beset so many units inherited from a different era. Further reports on these experiments should provide a guide to future action.

APPENDIX

Further Reading

Residential Care: A Select Bibliography
Compiled by Elizabeth Osborn, Librarian IRMR

(a) *Books*

1. Belknap, I. *Human Problems of a State Mental Hospital.* N.Y., McGraw-Hill, 1956.
2. British Psychological Society. *Children in Hospitals for the Subnormal. A Survey of Admissions and Educational Facilities.* BPS, 1966.
3. Clarke, A. M. and A. D. B. (eds.) *Mental Deficiency: the Changing Outlook*, 2nd ed. Methuen, 1965.
4. Dinnage, R. and Pringle, M. L. K. *Residential Child Care: Facts and Fallacies. A Review of Research in the U.K., U.S.A., Israel and Some Western European Countries between 1948–1966.* Longmans, 1967.
5. Edgerton, R. B. *The Cloak of Competence.* California University Press, 1967.
6. Goffman, E. *Asylums.* Anchor Press, 1963. [Chapter on the characteristics of the total institution.]
7. Moncrieff, J. *Mental Subnormality in London. A Survey of Community Care.* A Political and Economic Planning Report. PEP, 1966.
8. National Council of Social Service. *Committee of Enquiry. Caring for People: Staffing Residential Homes. A Report* . . . (Chairman: Professor Lady Williams, CBE). Allen & Unwin, 1967.
9. Norris, D. Some observations on the school life of severely retarded children. *J. Ment. Subnorm.*, Monog. Suppl., July 1968.
10. Saenger, G. *Factors influencing the Institutionalization of Mentally Retarded Individuals in N.Y. City. A Study of the Effect of Services, Personal Characteristics, and Family Background on the Decision to Institutionalize. A Report.* N.Y. State Interdepartmental Health Resources Board, 1960.
11. Stanton, A. and Schwartz, M. *The Mental Hospital.* N.Y., Basic Books, 1954.
12. Tizard, J. *Community Services for the Mentally Handicapped.* OUP, 1964. [Pt. 3: The education and care of mentally subnormal children.]

13. TIZARD, J. and GRAD, J. *The Mentally Handicapped and Their Families. A Social Survey*. Institute of Psychiatry (Maudsley Monograph No. 7). OUP, 1961.
14. WESSEX REGIONAL HOSPITAL BOARD. *Provision of Future Accommodation for the Mentally Subnormal*. Report of the Working Party. Winchester, WRHB, 1966.
15. WOOLF, P. G. The subnormality hospital and its role with physically handicapped children. Spastics Society. Education Seminar, Oxford, April 1968, p.8 (unpublished).

(b) *Government Publications*

16. MINISTRY OF HEALTH. Health and welfare. The development of community care. Plans for the Health and Welfare Services of the Local Authorities in England and Wales. Cmnd. 1973, HMSO, 1963, *with* Revision to 1973–74, HMSO, 1964, Revision to 1975–76, Cmnd. 3022, HMSO, 1966.
17. MINISTRY OF HEALTH. A hospital plan for England and Wales. Cmnd. 1064, HMSO, 1962, *with* Revised version covering the years 1972/73, HMSO, 1963, Revised version covering years 1973/74, HMSO, 1964.
18. MINISTRY OF HEALTH. Improving the effectiveness of the hospital service for the mentally subnormal. Issued with HM (65) 104. Obtainable from the Dept. of Health and Social Security.

(c) *Articles*

Refer also to:

19. MENTAL RETARDATION ABSTRACTS, Q. **1** (1), Jan./Mar. 1964. Issued by National Clearinghouse for Mental Health Information, National Institute of Mental Health. Obtainable from Supt. of Documents, U.S. Government Printing Office, Washington, D.C. 20402. Sub. $3.75 p.a. (4 issues per year).
20. AXELROD, I. *et al.* Nursing care of the mentally retarded. (Chairman of Symposium no. 28). *Proc. 1st Cong. Int. Ass. Sci. Stud. Ment. Defic.*, Montpellier, 1967.
21. BARTON, R. Institutional neurosis: consideration, clinical features, and differential diagnosis of institutional neurosis. World Congr. Psychiat., Montreal, 1961.
22. BENSBERG, G. J. and BARNETT, C. D. Attendant personnel: their selection, training and role. *Ment. Retard. Abstr.* 1964, **1,** 154–69 (American approach).
23. BERG, J. M. and FOTHERINGHAM, J. B. Observations on community school facilities for the mentally retarded and admission to institutions in Ontario, 1954–63. *Canad. Med. Ass. J.* 1965, **92,** 465–8.
24. BERKSON, S., HERMELIN, B., and O'CONNOR, N. Physiological responses of normal and institutionalised mental defectives to repeated stimuli. *J. Ment. Defic. Res.* 1961, **5,** 30–39.
25. BONE, M. and SPAIN, B. The effect of the provision of community services

upon the demand for hospital care. *Proc. 1st Cong. Int. Ass. Sci. Stud. Ment. Defic.*, Montpellier, 1967.

26. BRANDON, M. W. G. A survey of 200 women discharged from a mental deficiency hospital. *J. Ment. Sci.* 1960, **106,** 355–70.
27. CAMPBELL, A. Comparison of family and community contact of mentally subnormal adults in hospitals and in local authority hostels. *Brit. J. Prev. Soc. Med.* 1968, **22,** 165–9.
28. CRAIB, M. F. and WOODWARD, M. A survey of 44 children admitted to the Fountain Group Hospital under the Mental Deficiency Act, and subsequently accepted educable. *J. Ment. Sci.* 1958, **104,** 115–22.
29. DUPONT, A. Home-care in treatment of the mentally retarded. Int. Congr. Pediat. Tokyo, 7–13 Nov. 1965, pp. 312–15.
30. FRANKEL, H. H. Some consideration of home-care and hospitalisation of mentally handicapped and emotionally disturbed children. *Comm. 2nd Cong. Nurop. Pedopsichiat.*, Rome, 1963, vol. 11, pt. 1, pp. 403–7.
31. GOODRICH, W. Recent researches in early family development and child personality. *3rd Inst. Prevent. Psychiat. Meeting, Iowa State Univ.* 21–22 Apr. 1961, pp. 1–30.
32. GRAD, J. and SAINSBURY, P. Evaluating the community psychiatric service in Chichester: results. *Milbank Mem. Fd. Quart.* 1966, **44** (1), Suppl. 246–78.
33. HOLT, K. Principles of child health as seen in the care of handicapped children. In Symposium on the Handicapped Child, *Proc. Roy. Soc. Med.* 1966, **59,** 135–50.
34. KAHAN, V. L. An enquiry into the reasons for admission of under five year olds to a mental subnormality hospital. *J. Ment. Sci.* 1961, **107,** 481–5.
35. KAHAN, V. L. Treatment of severely disturbed children: an experiment in residential management. *Lancet* 1963, **i,** 319–21.
36. KING, R. D. and RAYNES, N. V. An operational measure of inmate management in residential institutions. *Soc. Sci. Med.* 1968, **2,** 41–53.
37. KING, R. D. and RAYNES, N. V. Patterns of institutional care for the severely subnormal. *Amer. J. Ment. Defic.* 1968, **72,** 700–9.
38. KING, R. D. and RAYNES, N. V. Some determinants of patterns of residential care. *Proc. 1st Cong. Int. Ass. Sci. Stud. Ment. Defic.*, Montpellier, 1967.
39. KIRMAN, B. H. The hospital and the backward child. *Med. Wld.* July 1956, pp. 1–6.
60. KIRMAN, B. H. The place of the mentally retarded. *Brit. Med. J.* 1967, **ii,** 2 (1–5).
61. KUSHLICK, A. A community service for the mentally surnormal. *Soc. Pyschiat.* 1966, **1,** 73.
62. KUSHLICK, A. A method of evaluating the effectiveness of a Community Health Service. *Soc. Econ. Admin.* 1967, **1,** 29–48.
63. KUSHLICK, A. The Wessex Experiment—comprehensive care for the mentally subnormal. *Brit. Hosp. J. Soc. Serv. Rev.* 6 Oct. 1967.
64. KUSHLICK, A. The Wessex plan for evaluating the effectiveness of residential care for the severely subnormal. *Proc. 1st Cong. Int. Ass. Sci. Stud. Ment. Defic.*, Montpellier, 1967.

65. Kushlick, A. and Cox, G. R. The ascertained prevalence of mental subnormality in the Wessex Region on 1st July 1963. *Proc. 1st Cong. Int. Ass. Sci. Stud. Ment. Defic.*, Montpellier, 1967.
66. Lawson, D. The comprehensive hospital. In Symposium on the Handicapped Child, *Proc. Roy. Soc. Med.* 1966, **59,** 143.
67. Leck, I., Gordon, W. L. and McKeown, T. Medical and social needs of patients in hospitals for the mentally subnormal. *Brit. J. Prev. Soc. Med.* 1967, **21,** 115–21.
68. Lyle, J. G. The effect of an institution environment upon the verbal development of imbecile children. I. Verbal intelligence. *J. Ment. Defic. Res.* 1959, **3,** 122–8. II. Speech and language. *J. Ment. Defic.* 1960, **4,** 1–13. III. The Brooklands Residential Family Unit. *J. Ment. Defic. Res.* 1960, **4,** 14–23.
69. Lyle, J. G. Some factors affecting the speech development of imbecile children in an institution. *J. Child Pyschol. Psychiat.* 1960, **1,** 121–9.
70. MacAndrew, C. and Edgerton, R. B. The everyday life of institutionalised "idiots". *Hum. Org.* 1964, **23,** 312–18.
71. McKeown, T. and Leck. I. Institutional care of the mentally subnormal. *Brit. Med. J.* 1967, **3,** 573–6.
72. Mittler, P. Report of the Working Party on Subnormality (BPS English Division of Professional Psychologists: Educational and Clinical). *Bull. Brit. Psychol. Soc.* 1963, **16,** 53.
73. Mittler, P. and Castell, J. H. F. Hospital and community care of the subnormal. *Lancet* 1964, **i,** 873–5.
74. Mittler, P. and Woodward, M. The education of children in hospitals for the subnormal: a survey of admissions. *Dev. Med. Child. Neurol.* 1966, **8,** 16–25.
75. Oliver, B. E. Admissions to a new unit for adolescent females in a subnormality hospital. *J. Ment. Subnorm.* 1966, **12,** 66–72.
76. Pasamanick, B. Research on the influence of sociocultural variables upon organic factors in mental retardation. *Amer. J. Ment. Defic.* 1959, **64,** 316–22.
77. Pense, A. W. Institutionalizing a mentally retarded child. *N.Y. St. Gen. Pract. News*, Sept./Oct. 1959, pp. 10–12.
78. Pilkington, T. The changing subnormality hospital. *Brit. Hosp. J.* 3 Feb. 1967, pp. 1–3.
79. Primrose, D. A. A. Natural history of mental deficiency in a Hospital Group and the community it serves. *J. Ment. Defic. Res.* 1966, **10,** 159.
80. Raynes, N. V. and King, R. D. The measurement of child management in residential institutions for the retarded. *Proc. 1st Cong. Int. Ass. Sci. Stud. Ment. Defic.*, Montpellier, 1967.
81. Richards, B. W. Institutional care for the mentally retarded in Great Britain. *Canada's Ment. Health Suppl.* 1964, **39,** 1–9.
82. Richards, B. W. Intelligence survey of a mental deficiency Institution. *Brit. J. Med. Psychol.* 1955, **28,** 267–70.
83. Richards, B. W. Mental subnormality in the general hospital. *J. Ment. Subnorm.* 1964, **10,** 1–4.

84. Shapiro, A. The needs of mentally handicapped children. *J. Ment. Subnorm.* 1962, **8,** (15), 101.
85. Spencer, D. A. Serving the mentally subnormal. *Lancet* 1967, **i,** 899.
86. Stephen, E. and Robertson, J. Can institutional care improve? The Brooklands experiment, etc. *Spec. Educ.* 1966, **55** (54), 13–16.
87. Tizard, J. Institutional defectives. *Amer. J. Ment. Defic.* 1954, **59,** 158–65.
88. Tizard, J. Residential care for the mentally retarded. *Proc. 1st Cong. Int. Ass. Sci. Stud. Ment. Defic.*, Montpellier, 1967.
89. Tizard, J. Residential care of mentally handicapped children. *Proc. London Conf. Sci. Stud. Ment. Defic.*, 1962, p. 659 and *Brit. Med. J.* 1960, **i,** 1041–6.
90. Tizard, J. The scale and nature of inpatient care for the subnormal. Symposium on the Handicapped Child, *Proc. Roy. Soc. Med.* 1966, **59,** 147–9.
91. Tizard, J., King, R. D., Raynes, N. V. and Yule, W. The care and treatment of subnormal children in residential institutions. *Proc. 1st Int. Conf. Ass. for Spec. Educ.*, Eltham, London, 1966.

(d) *Research in Progress*

Abbreviations: '*At*', place where research was undertaken; '*Spon.*', financial sponsors; *Publ.*', published or publication.]

92. Barker, D. W. An examination of local authorities' plans of services for the mentally subnormal in the Manchester Region up to 1974. *At*: Dept. of Social Administration, University of Manchester.
93. Bayley, M. L. The care at home of the mentally subnormal. *At*: Department of Sociological Studies, University of Sheffield. *Spon.*: Nuffield Provincial Hospitals Trust.
94. Brookes, W. L. The subnormal child and society. *At*: Dept. of Education, Univ. of Nottingham.
95. Cunningham, R. C. Hospital community orientation in the practice of mental subnormality. *At*: Royal Albert Hospital, Lancaster.
96. Gunzburg, H. C. and Donaldson, M. The effects of a simulated home environment in a hospital. *At*: St. Margaret's Hospital, Birmingham. *Spon.*: St. Margaret's HMC.
97. Kahan, V. L. The residential treatment of psychotic and severely disturbed children. *At*: West Stowell House, nr. Marlborough, Wilts. *Spon.*: Oxford RHB 9.
98. Leck, I., Gordon, W. L. and McKeown, T. Medical and social needs of patients in hospitals for the mentally subnormal. *At*: Department of Social Medicine, The Medical School, University of Birmingham. *Spon.*: Nuffield Provincial Hospitals Trust. *Publ.*: *Brit. J. Prev. Med.* 1967, **21,** 115–21.
99. McKeown, T. and Leck, I. Institutional care of the mentally subnormal. *At*: Department of Social Medicine, Medical School, University of Birmingham. *Spon.*: Nuffield Provincial Hospitals Trust. *Publ.*: *Brit. Med. J.* 1967, **3,** 573–6.

100. Martin, F. M., Done, M. R. and Spain, B. Study of services for the mentally subnormal. *At*: NAMH. *Spon.*: Spastics Society and NSMHC.
101. Miles, L. and Craft, M. Patterns of care for the subnormal. *At*: Oakwood Park Hospital Conway, N. Wales. *Spon.*: RHB 11. *Publ.*: Pergamon Press, 1967.
102. Mittler, P. and Castell, J. H. F. Intelligence of patients in subnormality hospitals. *At*: Psychology Department, Birkbeck College, University of London and BPS. *Publ.*: *Brit. J. Psychiat.* 1965, **111,** 219–25.
103. Mittler, P. and Castell, J. H. F. Survey of adult admissions to subnormality hospitals and intelligence distribution. *At*: Psychology Department, Birkbeck College, University of London. *Publ.*: *Brit. J. Psychiat.* 1965, **111,** 219–35.
104. Mittler, P. and Castell, J. H. F. Survey of children under 16 years admitted to subnormality hospitals, and intelligence distribution. *At*: Psychology Department, Birkbeck College, University of London. *Publ.*: *Bull. Brit. Psychol. Soc.* 1963, **52.**
105. Mittler, P. and Woodward, M. Education of children in hospital for the subnormal. *At*: Psychology Department, Birkbeck College, University of London. *Publ.*: British Psychological Society, 1966.
106. Morris, P. *et al.* Caring for the subnormal in a sociological study of institutions for the mentally handicapped. *At*: Univ. of Essex, Sociology Department. *Spon.*: NSMHC. *Publ.*: In preparation for Routledge & Kegan Paul, 1969.
107. Morris, P., Sawyer, L., Mujib, S. and Cox, B. Caring for the subnormal: a study of institutions for the mentally subnormal in England and Wales. *At*: Sociology Department, University of Essex, and Borough Polytechnic, University of London. *Spon.*: NSMHC. *Publ.*: in press.
108. Moss, P. G. Local authority residential care for subnormal children. *At*: Department of Social Science, University of Liverpool and Lancashire C.C. *Publ.*: DPhil dissertation.
109. Raynes, N. V. and King, D. Research into residential child care. *At*: Dept. of Child Development, Institute of Education, University of London. *Publ.*: Mag. Resident. Child Care Assoc. (in press).
110. Rundle, A. T. and Sylvester, P. E. Influence of homes and hospital environment on the stature of mentally retarded children. *At*: St. Lawrence's Hospital, Caterham, Surrey.
111. Stephen, E. and Roberts, J. The care of mentally handicapped children in hospital: an experiment. *At*: Queen Mary's Hospital for Children, Carshalton, Surrey. *Spon.*: Assoc. Aid for Crippled Children.
112. Thorpe, J. D. and Bardecki, A. Comparison of day centre and institutionalised subnormals in terms of intellectual efficiency. *At*: The Manor Hospital, Epsom, Surrey. *Publ.*: in press.
113. Tizard, J. Investigation concerned with children in long-term care in residential institutions in order (a) to throw light on the differing patterns of care offered to "deprived" children in care of local authorities and to handicapped and sick children in long-term hospital care; (b) to analyse the factors which appear to be

responsible for these differences and (c) to study the effects upon the children. *At*: Department of Child Development, Institute of Education, University of London. *Publ.*: The structure of a Mental Deficiency Service. *Proc. Int. Copenhagen Cong. Sci. St. Ment. Retard.*, 1964, vol. 2, pp. 729–36 (16 refs.).